2016

Election

DEDICATION

I dedicate this book to all the people who stood in total confusion during the 2016 election and did not understand what was going on. I hope this book will shed some light on this election and clear up some of their confusion.

ACKNOWLEDGEMENT

I would like to acknowledge all the people who have tried to remain logical, fair, and truth seeking during this 2016 election. I also would like to acknowledge all the people who have been violently harassed, threatened and intimidated by the immense amount of bullying that is going on during this election. I would also like to acknowledge the people on both sides of this election who lost friendships and family ties for reasons they still don't understand. I would also like to acknowledge that a great deal of work, understanding, open mindedness and humility will be needed to gain any understanding of this rift.

PREFACE

The 2016 election was unlike any other presidential election we've ever had that I can remember. The violence, the ended friendships, the split marriages, the broken dating, the hostile workplace environments, the crying, the protests. These things had never happened before. I remember people said we don't discuss religion or politics because we might get into a fight and people didn't do it. But now this 2016 election brought something to the surface that was so polarizing and split America into 2 such divergent camps that I don't know if things will ever get back to "normal" after this election. And after long study I have concluded that the 2020 election will make the 2016 election look like a lovefest. I believe this book points out very clearly a very distinct and irreconcilable difference between the 2 sets of voters that has not been brought to light nor understood in a long time.

CONTENTS

Chapter 1
The 2016 Election
Once again, I am humbled by Nietzsche

This Election Year of 2016 has caused me to think much. I was amazed at the division and separation of people. The huge gulf between human beings. I heard a statistic that 10% of romantic relationships have broken up over the 2016 election. I don't believe that has ever happened to such a degree in any presidential election in over 200 years. I heard about a movement where wives were expected to withhold sex from their husbands if they didn't vote for Hillary Clinton. People were encouraged to protest in the streets, news shows had anchors asking the world to help overthrow an American President. How could these radically different people get along in the first place? Are they so different? And why did this election bring their irreconcilable differences to the surface? What made this election so different? People who had never registered to vote got registered and voted in this election. People crossed party lines in record numbers. People who voted twice democrat once in 2008 and again in 2012 suddenly voted republican in 2016. This has been by far the most polarizing election in history. We have an election with 2 sides and no common ground. 2 sides who can't understand each other and want nothing to do with each other. Or maybe they are beginning to understand each other and should have never been together in the first place?

Chapter 2
A distinct split, the Stark Divide is Greater than we Thought

The people of the United States no longer hold core valued in common. The Melting Pot is gone. There are two different countries that make up America. Now this fundamental difference may have been highlighted in the 2016 election between Trump and Clinton but the chasm between these 2 groups has always existed and has been highlighted very strongly in several polarizing events leading up to the 2016 election.

A. Trayvon Martin vs George Zimmerman. People either think that a vicious thug attacked a Hispanic man punching him in the face breaking his nose and knocked him down then jumped on him and was sitting on him pounding his head into the concrete when the Hispanic man managed to reach his gun and shot him off his chest saving his life. Or they think an evil, racist, white man, hunted down and shot an innocent 12-year-old black boy like a dog for nothing. Intelligent people look at this single event and come away with 2 different conclusions and argue with each other and insult each other about it. It is interesting to note that even the President of the United States commented on this case.

B. The Michael Brown shooting. People either think that a 6-foot 4-inch drug dealing, criminal bully, thug, punched a cop and tried to take his gun and justifiably got shot while charging the cop trying to kill him. Or obviously a completely different set of people believe with all their hearts that an innocent black boy was shot while his hands were up in the air, begging the cop, please don't shoot and surrendering to the cop. Again, people given the exact same information come away with 2 radically different conclusions. It is interesting to note news stories still show up explaining the tragedy of this murder and the president of the united states send officials to this case.

C. Black lives matter. People either think this is a peaceful group asking for the murder and racism against an abused people to stop and this group to be treated equally and fairly or that it is a terrorist organization which has no legitimate claims and is extremely unfair and racist itself.

D. The wage gap. Again, we have 2 distinct groups people either think that women are paid only 70% for doing the exact same job as men. Or the other group that thinks this is a complete lie and that we have a law for the past 50 years making this illegal and not a single example of this can be found. Again equally "intelligent" people look at the same thing, read the same data and come away with opposite conclusions.

E. Only whites can be racist. This statement also divides people into 2 distinct camps. One group says that racism can be expressed by any person or group and the other says only one group the one in power or institutions can be racist. This also has implications as if someone is anti-racist they can only be speaking about anti-white. And if they are fighting racism they cannot be fighting against anything but white. Again, this argument leads to 2 distinct sides against each other.

F. School Choice. One group thinks everyone should have a choice to what type of education they provide for their children that parents have the responsibility right and obligation to educate their children. And the other thinks the state society and government has the responsibility, right and obligation to educate its children. Another factor in this issue is one side thinks it would be unfair if a bad parent didn't educate their child as well as a better parent.

G. Equality is another topic that separates these two groups. One side feels that everyone should be equal in outcome no matter what. The other feels that no one is equal and if everyone has equal opportunities then we will have unequal outcomes. They also feel it is your right to be better than another if you work harder or have more talent.

H. Reparations are another topic which divides people into irreconcilable differences One group thinks that a group of people must be paid back for any harm done to them and the opposite group thinks everyone must take their lumps and start today with no pay back for past events that may have happened to your ancestors some would even argue that these events help your present situation so you are owed nothing and probably should even be grateful. 2 distinctly different views.

I, Social Justice. One sides thinks that this thing called social justice is about the most important thing to fight for and should be center of any organizations energy and the other side has no clue what is being proposed because justice is just called justice and anytime you need to alter the name of something it is distorted. Much like politically correct really means not correct. Just as Social Justice really means not justice.

J. Affirmative action one side knows that if the world was fair and everyone had equal opportunities that the work place should have equal or the same outcome. The other side knows that in the real world there will be some winners and some losers some people will get ahead and some will be left behind. When a black student who scores 700s on his SAT gets accepted into all 8 Ivy League schools one side sees that as a great success. The other side points out that no White or Asian student is accepted to half the Ivy League schools with SAT scores of 800 and sees that as terrible.

K. Illegal immigration. One group feels that every country has a right to have a border and protect its space and control who gets in. While the other group feels that people are all the same that there should be no borders or countries and no in or out groups. That nationality is unimportant and people should be free to move across borders as they see fit.

L. Welfare: One group feels it should feed, house, cloth, and take care of those who cannot do this for themselves and the other feels it is not their responsibility to feed, house, cloth and care for other people. Some even feel that by providing such care the misery of the problem is made worse. (This is a difference in intentions vs results.)

M. Gun Control this is another area which divides the country into separate groups. One group believes people should not have weapons that can kill other human beings and that it is the government's job to kill other human beings and to protect you. The other believes people should have weapons that can kill other human beings and that it is their duty to protect yourself and your family. This group also believes the government is not very good at much least of all protecting them from dangers.

N. The 2016 election with Donald Trump vs Hillary Clinton. Your side either thinks that the most qualified person to ever run for president is running against the most unqualified person to ever run for president. One who is also an evil racist, misogynistic, homophobic, xenophobic, bully, reality TV star liar and horrible person. Or on the opposite side you think a person who was not bribed and beholding to corporations and outside lobbyists and special interests someone who wants to be president of America, the only person who would actually sacrifice wealth to become president. Finally, a person who wants what's best for America, who wants to put America first and really wants to make America great again. A person who is going to drain the swamp, someone who is brave and fights back when attacked and who is not a coward and doesn't back down to bullying is running against the most corrupt evil lying inept traitorous vile politician to ever run for president. This was not an election like many in the past when a significant percent of the population really didn't think there was much difference in the 2 candidates.

Chapter 3
Not a matter of intelligence

What is the difference between these 2 groups? As I listened to somewhat intelligent people make what I thought to be blatantly untrue statements I wondered how intelligent they were. It is easy to just assume they are intelligent people lying which would make them smart and evil. However, in many cases I think they believed their statements were factual. I started to question the very definition of intelligence.

I had always thought that if people given facts cannot interpret those facts correctly and come to a true, logical and accurate conclusion they must not be very intelligent. So, I first assumed that the other side was just stupid but I knew several smart people on both sides of this election. And this puzzled me. I think if I gave an IQ test to the 60 million people who voted for Trump and the same IQ test to the 60 million people who voted for Clinton that I would not get any strong correlation one direction or the other. It is not as if the voters who voted for Clinton or Trump have an IQ of 85 and the opposite side have an IQ of 115. How can this be? If a person given facts or input data cannot come to a real rational conclusion and this cannot be repeated i.e. duplicated than what is intelligence?

I even began to formulate a new theory of intelligence and hypothesized that some people just had a higher level of tolerance for cognitive dissonance or are less annoyed by hypocrisy. Maybe intelligence is not tied as strongly to being able to discern the truth as I thought. Could a person's ability to find the truth be unrelated to intelligence? Most IQ tests which have a pattern of symbols started and a person must find the true one that fits in the pattern or logically comes next would seem to be a measure of a person's ability to find the truth or discern the truth. One would think that given a series of facts people with a given IQ would come to the same conclusion. However, this is not what happens something more is going on. I thought about the people who believe the world is 6,000 years old or that blowing themselves up with infidels will get them 72 virgins. In both these cases and many others, emotions have highjacked thinking. I have heard arguments by creationists who are brilliant, using every conceivable argument and angle about laws of physics and laws of chemistry and laws of biology showing why the earth is only 6,000 years old. Their arguments are brilliant, and intelligent, far more creative than I could ever come up with.

Thinking is only a small part of our brain, which sits on a large part of our brain the emotional mass. But why are some people so different emotionally about this 2016 election? Why do some people have to adjust all their thinking, and reasoning to fit their emotions and why do their emotions force them to "think" a certain way? Once I dismissed the idea that the other side was just "stupid" or "evil" I wondered what driving force split America into two separate camps. I thought about this and finally I did get an insight when I remembered that Nietzsche had already answered all my questions long ago.

Chapter 4
Two different groups

As can be seen by this list that there are 2 distinct, radically different types of people living in the United States today and there really is no common ground. Each opposite side sees the other as completely wrong, completely lacking objectivity, logic and fairness. They think the other side has no limit for hypocrisy. That they are liars, bullies, criminals and want the destruction of their group. I thought how is that possible? How can people given the exact same information, the exact same facts, come up with exactly the opposite conclusion? What is it that panics one side so much about this election? Now physical attacks done by one side to the other in this election are considered normal?

It is truly a case when one side does not and cannot understand the other. Riots, burnings, lootings, protests, hitting people in the head, knocking them down stomping on them. This is on any YouTube video for all to see. Are we in a situation where the basic foundational morality and belief system of people are so against each other that they cannot live in peace anymore? One part of society thinks you can vote for a despicable, hate filled, dishonest, dangerous, bigot with bad hair or you can vote for Trump. And the other side thinks you can vote for a despicable, hate filled dishonest dangerous bigot with bad hair or vote for Hillary. There is even a term for the people who have such a different view of Trump then others it's called TSD Trump Derangement Syndrome describing people who think all previous presidents were good, honest, smart, kind people and Trump is uniquely evil, dishonest, dumb and mean.

I think I now see the answer to my question of why 2 different sides given identical facts have come up with 2 opposite, diametrically opposed conclusions, viewpoints, and paradigms. How can logical intelligent educated people seeking the truth given identical facts come to such diametrically opposed opposite conclusions. The answer like so often is the case was in my question. Yes, there are 2 different sides of 2 different people who want 2 different things and both cannot exist together. One will grow only at the expense of the other.

Chapter 5
Rescue by Nietzsche

The Great Nietzsche answered my question many years ago. Nietzsche said that there are two fundamentally different ways of being, thinking, acting, behaving, and seeing the world. Basically, two fundamental types of morality. One Nietzsche called Master morality' and the other he called 'Slave morality'. For this paper, I will call one slave morality and the other free morality or one r-selected and the other K-selected I will sometimes refer to one as the Left and the other as the Right.

Nietzsche said that originally all morality was simple and everyone had the same morality. What was beneficial and had a good result was what was good. Those things that were good were the traits people admired. The best of people, the best traits, the best of virtues, the best of qualities, that was good. These traits would have been the classic traits any child admires in a super hero. Strong, brave, kind, noble, generous, smart, overcoming great odds, a winner, etc. but as people became civilized and victimized and people became enslaved society became stratified the idea of a hero became farther and farther removed from the common man. As the Roman Empire spread and religion spread and many people became serfs or vassals or slaves a new type of morality emerged. A new way of thinking that made the state of a slave as a good thing, as a natural way of being, so Nietzsche said we have developed two types of Morality. The old Master morality and this new way of thinking which he called Slave morality. I will try to explain, compare and contrast these two ways of seeing the world as simply as possible. I would bet many people can be placed into the categories Nietzsche called Slave morality or Master Morality. Based on their feelings, opinion and viewpoints from about a dozen events that have polarized America in the last few years. With Clinton, you had a woman who wanted to do things for you, to protect you, who promised to protect the weak, who would fight to give privileges to the underprivileged, who promised to fight for social justice, who offered to remove borders, who said women would finally get paid the same as a man for the same work. V.s a man seen as a winner, an achiever who promised to make us great again who would help us compete who promised to level the playing field. The Master mentality or Morality people could not help but be attracted to Trump and the Slaves who needed victims and oppressors could not help but be attracted to Clinton. Attacks by the left on Trump made him stronger with his supporters because they want the strong unapologetic warrior who attacks his enemies. The left could not understand how a man could fight back and be considered "Good" This was just advertising to his fans and a conformation that he was fit to lead. Whereas to the left it was proof he was unfit to lead. Trump would say things that the Left thought should destroy him then gasped in horror when it just made him stronger. It was like Trump fans were different than Clinton fans. The same thing took place with the Trayvon Martin case. The left could not stand a man who defended himself, who defended his neighborhood, who actually gasp, carried a gun. The worst things a man can do according to slave morality is "Stand your ground" a slave can never stand his ground and anyone who does is hated and resented by those with slave morality. I talked to several Left people who even admitted that George Zimmerman got a fair trial and agreed with the outcome but they always said. But that stand your ground law needs to change. Now the fact that the stand your ground law never came up in the case is evidence that we have 2 different ways to thinking how dare someone legally can stand their ground? The Michael Brown shooting is another separation of people. A cop shot a man who by all facts punched him and was trying to kill him the cop refused to be overpowered to be a victim. In slave morality, you have no choice but to be a victim, so being a victim is a good thing. To refuse to be a victim of a big, strong, brutal guy attacking you is heresy. Again, this shows the divide and distinction between slave morality and master morality. Another dividing topic is BLM the most joyous thing a slave can hear is the big bad system is stacked against the oppressed group who are powerless to help themselves. For a group to be singled out as victims, for them to be treated unfairly that they are persecuted, that they are bullied, is the paradigm those with slave morality want to hear it justifies their existence their value and their belief. And anyone who denies this is basically denying the very God of Slave morality. The same is with the wage gap. Those of Slave Morality quote the statistic that if you add up all the pay men receive and all the pay women receive that women only make 70% of the pay men make. They then say how this proves men and women get paid differently for the exact same job. While the ones of Master Morality take this fact, and think well if you average in all the people who start businesses like Bill Gates and Steve Jobs and Sam Walton and Mark Zuckerberg etc. and all the people who work 70-hour weeks trying to sell the extra real estate or make partner in the firm or become the president or CEO. And you compare those to the women who work part time or take off in the middle of their career to have children or who while working don't work the overtime because they choose to see their kids plays or want to be home at night with their families then of course averaging in all the men with all the women in amerce would show a pay gap which is expected fair and right. But even if you look at the Data more closely and it shows that only comparing women who have never married and had kids with men who have never married and had kids and if this Data shows those women out earn their male counter parts. This still means nothing to the left those with slave morality. They must constantly be in slave mode. They must have, they absolutely require an oppressed group, an enslaved group. Even if you show that the equal pay act in 1963 made it illegal to pay women less for the same job this means nothing. Even if you show that all teachers' firemen businesses etc. have a single pay scale not a male and female pay scale this means nothing. The falsehood of the Michael Brown hands up don't shoot is apparent to anyone. The falsehood of the gender pay gap is apparent for anyone but even Hillary Clinton on her campaign for president in 2016 said it's about time a woman makes the same pay as a man. As if this enslavement of women was still a problem. These are only 5 examples but they show that there is no middle ground between these two philosophies.

Chapter 6
Master Morality

Master Morality weighs actions on a scale of good or bad consequences or results unlike slave morality which weighs actions on a scale of good or evil intentions. This is a chasm of difference between the two groups of people as one will look at a social program to combat a problem such as homelessness, drug addiction, education, hunger, crime etc. and ask what the results are what are the consequences of the program. While those with a Slave mentality incorporating Slave, Morality will look at what are the intentions of the program which to them weighs more heavily than the results. In Master Morality, the value or nonvalue of an action is derived solely from its results, and zero from its intentions. Whereas in Slave morality the intentions of the program are of paramount importance while the results are not their fault or responsibility. There are many other examples where these two opposed ways of being come into conflict. One of the most striking examples of this is luck or fate or as it was called in ancient days the favor of the gods. A person of Master Morality would never curse his fate or believe anything that happened to him was not his own responsibility. When Beowulf went to battle a dragon or Grendel he always said let fate decide. If Achilles or Batas or Siegfried slipped on a rock or broke a leg or got bit by a dragon or hit by a bolt of lightning or whatever happened to them fair or unfair they accepted this as their fault and their fate. They fought on despite any bad luck. In the Sacred Havamal it says a strong man can twist his fate and overcome his fate even going against what the Norms decree. Whereas the person who has adopted Slave Morality, Slave Ethics throws his arms up and says this is beyond me. This is unfair, this is not my fault I cannot be expected to overcome obstacles someone else is obligated to save me. Master morality is the classic Morality which values those traits of the traditional father, the nobleman, the chieftain, the clan leader. In other words, the Hero, which included the desirable traits such as

1. **Achievement** is good to be admired to be emulated worked for and is the highest good. In Slave Morality Achievement is only gained on the backs of slaves so is suspect and to be ridiculed and looked down upon. The very idea of taking a chance starting a business trying to get ahead achieve more gain freedom is heresy to those with slave morality. They must tax, destroy, redistribute, wealth and knock those down. They must have equal outcomes. And the Master mentality people must remove obstacles to achievement success and rising above the herd. They want equal opportunities a fair contest but they want unequal outcomes whereas those with Slave Morality want equal outcomes even if this requires unequal opportunities.
2. **Beauty** is good it is to be admired what is beauty is completely different between these two ways of thinking. In slave morality, the ugly is to be extoled Art can be anything a bucket of Urine or modern Art is an example of slave morality. A grotesque fat person is to be admired and not fat shamed. A person so fat they are at risk of death and who cannot move very well is to be admired as much as a muscular fit person who has sacrificed and worked hard to look good.

3. Courage is one of the up most valuable traits in Master Morality. In Slave Morality Courage is not only useless, it gets you killed. But to a free man taking his chances, fighting obstacles, in his conquest for success courage is so admired.

4. Favor of the gods or Luck. This was considered one of the greatest's traits of the Hero who was born strong healthy better than others. In Slave Morality, this is considered evil, unfair and wrong. All must be equal. This is so important in slave culture that even if everyone only got half a cup of beans a day that would be preferable to some getting steak and some getting one cup of beans.

5. Generosity this trait was a virtue of the rich and powerful but one with Slave Morality can only be generous if they persuade their master to give something away. Notice how modern leftists want to force others through taxes to give but rarely open their own homes to the homeless or live in neighborhoods with them.

6. Hard work is a noble trait for a person with Master Morality to win battles to acquire more slaves to increase his holdings but a slave that works hard is just a chump a sucker.

7, Kindness is something only a master can express. A slave cannot really even express kindness. A master can give you a day off or offer mercy and give something of value. A slave expressing kindness is wasting his time. Therefore, Nietzsche said those with master morality are kinder than those with slave morality. It can also be seen from this as who is kinder and gentler at the rallies and protests.

8. Intelligence there might be no other trait that separates those with slave morality from those with master morality more than their stance on intelligence. Slave minded people hate the very concept of IQ, test scores, or any objective, reproducible reliable method of scoring, measuring or assessing intelligence. To someone with master morality intelligence is of upmost importance. Intelligence allows you to make good choices. A slave does not have many choices. Intelligence allows you to expand your options and defeat enemies. Those with slave mentality hate IQ tests or the very concept or discussion of IQ. This should come as no surprise as a reliable reproducible consistent system which measured people's ability and talent putting them at different levels and separating them is about the most horrid thing imaginable to one with slave morality. Whereas those with the mindset of a free man say of course different people have different intelligence it's a simple trait like height or weight and just as easily observed.

9. Luck is another trait that the free man values but the slave does not. Luck to a free man is the sum of all his skills. Luck is only when preparation meets opportunity. Luck means the gods favor you, that you had good parents that you come from a good family line. To a slave luck is something to despise.

10. Overcoming is a trait of upmost value. The power strength the resolve the skill to overcome adversity, circumstance to make your own luck these are traits a free man values most highly and what a slave despises

11. Results perhaps no other trait separates those
with slave morality and those with master morality
more that Results a free man only cares about the
results a slave only cares about intentions. I have
heard almost every liberal finally say in the defense of
a failed program that "the intentions were good" even
if the war on poverty caused more poverty the war on
illegitimate fathers caused more illegitimate fathers no
matter what the miserable results. The r-selected
slave morality people will always end any discussion
about social programs with "the intentions were good"

12. Risk taking this trait is similar to winning. Just as
the risk associated with winning or losing is desirable
to the free man and abhorrent to slaves. So is all risk
taking, the one with slave morality does not want any
risk, any danger, any discomfort. By contrast a free
man does not avoid risk in his quest for glory.

13. Skill is a trait valued by the free man but if a
slave has skill it does him no good. Skill is something
a free man uses for his own benefit but skill to a slave
is just something he uses for another person's benefit.
A slave who has great skill or talent is only taken
advantage of more. A slave who can pick 100 bushels
of corn is in no better of a situation than a slave who
can pick 50 bushels of corn. Whereas a free man who
owns his farm who can pick twice as much corn as his
neighbor is in a great situation. It can be seen from
this example that slave ethics or slave morality is
going to be vastly different from free man or master
morality. As a free man is master of himself and not a
slave.

14. Strength the slave and the freeman look at strength in opposite directions a freeman wants strength to accomplish his goals a slave wants to use the strength of others to do something for him.

15. Success again we see the opposite reaction from these two diametrically opposed groups to a free man success is a result of his superiority and to a slave success or rather his lack of success is a result of his inferiority.

16. Winning again the contrast between the slave and the master is readily apparent with this trait. The liberal modern age has no winners and no losers everyone gets a trophy the participation trophy is present and there are no winners and no losers. The free man wants to win and does not think you can win unless you have the risk of losing.

Chapter 7
Slave morality

Nietzsche described slave morality as a mutation of the classic virtues. It arose from the new and huge emerging class of people who were now slaves. They had no power, no sovereignty, no say, and no control over their fate. To these people the old classic Morality was not an option they developed a new morality which Nietzsche called Slave Morality. As can been seen this new way of living which produced a new type of human who was a slave had to acquire a new type of thinking. A new set of virtues, new types of values, a new type of morality. This had several effects. The new morality this new way of thinking, believing, and living valued such things as

1. Acceptance A slave has no choice but to accept his station, his captivity, his low station, he should not work to make it better or overcome anything. If anything is going to get better only his master the government can make it so. Nothing h

2. Bad luck a slave has bad luck. If a slave had good luck or favor of the gods it made him less equal to the other slaves which is a bad thing. By definition a slave winding up as a slave proves his luck is bad. So, slaves don't admire good luck, good fortune, or having the favor of the gods.

3. Conformity is a virtue as a slave. To stand out from the crowd to gain glory is a threat so conformity became a virtue. No slave wants to draw attention to himself. No slave wants to stand out from the crowd. What does the biggest, strongest, smartest, most beautiful slave get? More work, more exploitation and more abuse. The best strategy for a slave is to conform and fit into the herd.

4. Dependence or Dependency a slave's life is dependent of his master's wishes treatment he is not independent so this new situation forced upon him becomes a virtue.

5. Equality and Equal outcomes this is a goal of the slave who want all people who try to get the same result this is a goal of affirmative action that all people regardless of skill have equal outcomes. This can even be seen in countries where the income gap or wage gap or any gap is considered bad. In a country where everyone makes between 1,000 and 2,000 dollars a year is considered much better than a country where everyone makes between 20,000 and 1,000,000 dollars a year. Because even if 99% live better in the rich country it's still less equal.

6. Getting along this is a goal of the r-selected to follow the herd and not stand out from the herd to be unnoticed to not be a shining hero but to be in the group.

7. Having an oppressor the slave must have an oppressor to have any identity. A free man does not have an oppressor. A slave must justify his position his existence and even define himself through an oppressor.

8. Helplessness the natural state of a slave is being helpless to be too weak to fight an oppressor being helpless being bullied being unable to defend yourself is a virtue. Those who would not fight back and love their enemies.

9. Herd mentality a slave must fit into the herd he must not stand out or above the rest. A slave who has great talent or is superior is just an object of scorn or hatred fitting into the herd and being like everyone else is a virtue.

10. Intentions to a slave, intentions have replaced results as a virtue. It does not matter what the results are to a slave it is only the intentions that matter. A slave who is too weak to do anything can show his virtue by is intentions. A slave signals his morality by his intentions because a slave is not responsible for his results.

11. Lack of results would be a horrible disgrace to a free man one who is master of himself. But a slave he is not responsible for his own success or the success of any plan he makes so the lack of results is minor compared to his intentions.

12. Losing to a slave is out of his control the game is stacked against him he has already lost and will by fate or luck or privilege loose again so a slave must be protected from losing and everyone must get a trophy.

13. Misfortune this quality is similar to losing. A slave is a product of misfortune. By definition a slave has misfortune and could do nothing about it. Otherwise he would be a free man. Freemen have misfortunes but they overcome them. Freemen are bigger than their misfortunes whereas slaves are not. Anyone who is not misfortunate is not a slave and not one of the crowd not one of the herd. The most misfortunate among the slaves is actually the one displaying a trait worth admiring and paying tribute to. Caring for and focusing on and glorifying the most misfortunate is something those with slave mentality would do.

14. Nice I heard this many times, during the election even by smart people. Hillary is Nice, Trump is mean. As if that is a way to pick a leader. Not even if it was true. Because I think you could make the point that Hillary is very mean I don't think by any objective measurements you could say that Trump was meaner than Hillary or Hillary was nicer than Trump but it was this perception. Those with slave morality cannot stand if their leader might be mean. Another thing about this if you are a slave the greatest thing you can have is a nice master but if you are a free man you want your master to be fierce, strong, smart and at least could be mean. Every football player talks about the meanest coach he ever had with reverence. Every soldier talks about the meanest drill sergeant he had with reverence. The free man who owns himself and is master of himself will talk about those tough, mean coaches. It is interesting that one of my personally biggest pieces of evidence that Trump would be a better president than Clinton was the fact that Indiana University Coach Bobby Knight and Purdue Coach Gene Keady and Notre Dame Coaches Digger Phelps and Lou Holtz all said that Trump was their pick. Now those 4 distinct different men have a large amount of experience and success at recognizing talent outcomes. And none are concerned with Niceness.

15. Safety above all a slave desires safety after all this is what a slave has traded his freedom for. If a slave risked everything to become free he would not be a slave so by his very essence a slave is a product of clinging to safety. Even if it is an illusion.

16. Stupidity again we see the difference in morality a brilliant talented above the herd slave is not of value. The stupid are just as valuable as the intelligent to one with slave morality

17. Sympathy this is of great importance to the slave culture, sympathy is agreement with your situation where as a free man might break the bottle over an alcoholic's head or stab a heroin junkie with his own needle a weak slave would agree that drugs are too strong for his friend to beat and agree to have sympathy for the loser to week and enslaved by drugs.

18. Tolerance is like sympathy a free man a master will not tolerate those who deviate from greatness whereas a slave has to tolerate all the trash, slings arrows, misfortunes, and luck, life throws at him.

19. Ugliness there is no greater example of the chasm between slave and master morality than modern art. This idea that everything is equally valuable equally beautiful and has equal merit is a virtue to those with slave morality but a foreign idea to a free sovereign individual

20. Victimhood to a slave being a victim is a natural state, a good thing if you are not a victim you are probably an oppressor, a master a free man and that is a very bad thing.

21. Weakness a slave almost by definition is weaker than his master subservient to his oppressor it is a virtue to be weak. To defend the weak to glorify the weak. To be strong and resilient self-reliant is again to make you one of the oppressors which is not a good trait according to slave morality.

As can be seen this 2016 election which caused such shock and awe, surprise and confusion was simply due to two very different types of mind sets. Totally different people living in the same society the same country and trying to choose the leader who represents them.

Chapter 8
Beta males, feminists, and protected ones

This is another area which divides these two groups, i.e. the trump voter and Clinton voter. The beta male is by definition, a 2nd class male. Almost by definition the alpha male is in the minority. And while it may have been true in the past that a majority of men were not the alpha male, they certainly were strong, noble, brave, honorable, men who aspired to be the alpha male and were at least seeking, working toward and admired those traits and caricaturists. That is not the case today. The only way for a weak, lazy, stupid, untalented, male to gain any status, recognition, or power is to become a victim. Or he can join in a rally in support victims. It is interesting that these men at the feminist rallies are gaining more access to females than a real high-quality male would. I had an old student come back to me and he laughed about attending one of the Hillary Clinton rallies and I said why and he smiled and said a guy has to do what he has to do to get laid. Now he was very right wing's political views and was a political science major at college but he knew if you wanted to gain access to females he had to act with slave morality not master morality. The same can be said for the feminists I have seen an unattractive female who could not get dates or much social recognition decide she was transgender and really a man her social status shot up dramatically by claiming to be a victim she rallied to support of many people, who would've ignored or otherwise. The greatest accomplishment of a slave minded person is not to become free but to become a protected class to become the house slave and not the field slave because that slave is now in a very cushy position. So, it should come as no surprise when we have 2 distinctly different groups of people who have 2 distinct ways of looking at life. The goal of those with slave morality is to become the protected class. While those with master morality want to go out and slay the dragon, fight the enemy, win the glory, risk death and win. The people with slave morality want to be the protected ones, the ones who don't ever have to risk anything, the ones who never have to fight, who have all of the fighting done for them. Again, we have very distinct, divergent, different, groups of people who in no way shape or form can find any common ground yet expect them to peacefully life together always with one at the expense of the other. Those with master morality want to be the hero, want to overcome challenges, want to face adversity, and succeed with their own power. And those with slave morality the Beta males, the feminists, and the others who want to join some protected group who only want to avoid all those things and have the fighting done for them.

I don't want to imply that certain races or sexes have one or the other way of thinking. Anyone can have one way of thinking or the other. A homosexual can be a hero who is brave and strong. Anyone can want to start a business, take risks, face challenges. A person of any race, creed, religion, color, etc. who has master morality, who wants to be the hero, who wants to overcome those odds can have that way of thinking all the way down to their core being. It is interesting to note how much these types of people are hated by the left. The ones who could cash in on slave morality but don't want to are attacked and despised the most.

The slave mentality, the slave morality is being marketed and sold to everyone and some people take up, they even vote for it, they are even drawn to it politically. And some people are repulsed by it and vote against it and are not drawn to it politically. I don't see any way for these 2 groups of people will never find common ground. For one will always live at the expense of the other.

One famous example of this is the cuttlefish in a mating strategy the biggest, strongest, most colorful males, the alpha males display and fight with each other at the bottom of the sea floor for the female's attention. This strategy works out pretty well, because the healthiest, most fit sets of genes are sent to the next generation. The best fighters will likely be the best swimmers and the cuttlefish offspring who are born from this pairing will have an advantage. However, some sneaky beta male cuttlefish who have no ability to beat the alpha males in a fair fight have learned to tuck in their tentacles and appear like a female. They swim right by the male regarding his territory and while pretending to be a female take a position among the other females waiting to see the winner of the fight and make with the females while the stronger males fight each other. This is an incredibly effective way to bypass the risky system of competing on a level playing field and for those weaker members of the species to successfully mate.

Another example of this in the animal kingdom was among a certain species of tree frog. This situation was even more, complicated. The alpha male frogs would beat up the week beta male frogs and chased them out of their territory so the beta males had no way of mating. But in the population, there appeared a super male variety. In the super males were so big and strong they could beat up the alpha males and monopolize access to all the females. However, as nature would have it the small week beta males could act enough like females that the super males did not recognize them and they would breed the females very successfully. Field researchers noted a rock paper scissors game in the frog reproduction competition. Alpha males would be dominant until a super male showed up who was able to beat them and gain access to all the females who would remain dominant until beta males show up and gain access to the females reading them out of existence until an original alpha male type which show up and become the dominant strategy.

This chapter shows that there is no best strategy between slave morality and master morality. It is simply 2 types of strategy that can be employed to be successful in life. It is easy for one type of person to look at the other type of person and think they are wrong. But if you are weak and dumb and a coward and have no ability to compete with smarter stronger more courageous people having slave morality is much more useful to you that having master morality.

Chapter 9
Quotes by Nietzsche

In this chapter, I have haphazardly grabbed quotes from Nietzsche from a scattering of his works, in an attempt to show the reader Nietzsche's message about slave morality vs master morality. I tried to cite the work when convenient but really don't care about scholarship if these words don't move or awaken you there is nothing much extra I can do for you.

Everything that elevates an individual above the herd is called evil by those with Slave Morality.
Everything that elevates an individual above the herd is called good by those with Master Morality.
Those with Master Mentality feel anyone who separates himself from the herd though great luck talent or skill is to be admired.
Those with Slave Mentality feel anyone who separates himself from the herd though great luck talent or skill is to be pulled back down into the herd.
Nietzsche said vanity is the hallmark of the meek and powerlessness. There must always be an approving reinforcing master to give them praise or value so slave seek out the praise and approval. The slave morality is subject to flattery--such persons know they do not deserve praise yet they believe it when they are praised by the master since they have not the abilities to create value. Vanity is a consequence of inferiority. Nietzsche believed the person with slave morality would become rancorous and poison himself becoming neither truthful nor ingenuous nor honest and forthright with himself. Speaking of tolerance all the while not tolerating any other views.

Nietzsche said, On the Genealogy of Morals: A Polemical Tract, First Essay: Good and Evil

"When the oppressed, the downtrodden, the conquered say to each other, with the vengeful cunning of the powerless, "Let us be different from evil people, namely, good! And that man is good who does not overpower, who hurts no one, who does not attack, who does not retaliate, who hands revenge over to God, who keeps himself hidden, as we do, who avoids all evil and demands little from life in general—like us, the patient, humble, and upright"—what that amounts to, coolly expressed and without bias, is essentially nothing more than "We weak people are in fact weak. It's good if we do nothing, of which we are not capable of, because we are not strong enough." But this bitter state, this shrewdness of the lowest ranks, which even insects possess (for in great danger they stand as if they were dead in order not to do "too much"), has, thanks to the counterfeiting and self-deception of powerlessness, dressed itself in the splendor of a self-denying, still, patient virtue, just as if the weakness of the weak man himself, that means his essence, his actions, his entire single, inevitable, and irredeemable reality, is a voluntary achievement, something willed, chosen, an act, something of merit. This kind of man needs to believe in the disinterested, freely choosing "subject" out of his instinct for self-preservation, self-approval, in which every falsehood is habitually sanctified. The subject (or, to use a more popular style, the soul) has up to now probably been the best principle for belief on earth, because, for the majority of the dying, the weak, and the downtrodden of all sorts, it makes possible a sublime self-deception which establishes weakness itself as freedom and their being like this or that as something meritorious."

Nietzsche said
"That lambs are annoyed at the great predatory birds is not a strange thing, and it provides no reason for holding anything against these large birds of prey, because they snatch away small lambs. And if the lambs say among themselves "These predatory birds are evil—and whoever is least like a predatory bird—and especially who is like its opposite, a lamb—shouldn't that animal be good?" there is nothing to find fault with in this setting up of an ideal, except for the fact that the birds of prey might look down with a little mockery and perhaps say to themselves "We are not at all annoyed with these good lambs—we even love them. Nothing is tastier than a tender lamb."

Nietzsche said in Twilight of The Idols or How One Philosophizes with a hammer,

"To call the taming of an animal its "improvement" sounds almost like a joke to our ears. Whoever knows what goes on in farms, zoos, and menageries doubts that the beasts are "improved" there. They are weakened, they are made less harmful, and through the depressive effect of fear, through pain, through wounds, and through hunger, they become sickly beasts. It is no different with the tamed man whom the priest has "improved." In the early Middle Ages, when the church was indeed, above all, a menagerie, the most beautiful specimens of the "blond beast" were hunted down everywhere; and the noble Teutons, for example, were "improved." But how did such an "improved" Teuton who had been seduced into a monastery look afterward? Like a caricature of man, like a miscarriage: he had become a "sinner," he was stuck in a cage, imprisoned among all sorts of terrible concepts. And there he lay, sick, miserable, malevolent against himself, full of hatred against the springs of life, full of suspicion against all that was still strong and happy. In short, a "Christian." "Physiologically speaking: in the struggle with beasts, to make them sick may be the only means for making them weak. This the church understood: it ruined man, it weakened him--but it claimed to have "improved" him."

Today it might be it a Hollywood actress or celebrity or political correctness or group think. This is one thing that the left with its Slave morality missed entirely. If the beautiful, popular celebrity, the master of what to think said it is good all would fall in line with what is good. But those with Master mentality are repulsed by this. Those with Slave Morality follow the Hollywood chosen like groupies, like slaves as worshippers while those with Master Morality are repulsed by this. The same is with the main stream media. If the established authority says it was so then those with Slave Mentality must follow. The shock and disillusion of the Trump victory when all of Hollywood, and all the Television, all of media, all the masters said it was not to be so was unthinkable to those with Slave morality. How could a human go against what the Masters said? To stand alone against the powerful, the ones in charge, is unthinkable to those with slave morality.

Another difference is with Slave Morality there must always have an oppressor and the oppressed. Without a master, the slave has no value. A slave does not exist without his master. The slave owes his very existence, his very definition on there being a master or in modern days an oppressed and an oppressor. In slave morality, we have a thing called social justice which has become so much more important than real justice. The meek, weak, downtrodden are to be focused on and glorified. Those of the lowest value are now of the utmost value. Brains, courage, creativity, hard work, overcoming or any of the classic virtues these have been replaced by slave virtues

Nietzsche believed slave morality led to the objective of all human arrangements is through distracting ones thought to cease to be aware of life we can see this today in the most trivial aspects of pop culture. Nietzsche said for a man to achieve greatness he must ask questions and ponder on questions the herd is too weak and stupid to ask. Nietzsche also said religion was an opiate of the masses and he never even drank alcohol to avoid its narcotic effects nor even sweet drinks as he was not a slave to his taste buds but only water or milk so far did he carry this belief of taking control of his life.

Nietzsche said, "For strong-willed men, the 'good' is the noble, strong, and powerful, while the 'bad' is the weak, cowardly, timid, and petty. Those with master morality do not have to construct their happiness fictitiously by looking at their enemies, their oppressors, their masters, as all those with slave morality rancorous men are wont to do, they must have an oppressor a blame someone who is stronger, better off or master over them. This stands in utter contrast to Master morality which values pride, strength, and nobility, freedom, self-reliance, courage, overcoming, conquering However Slave Morality requires a scapegoat, a master, an oppressor, a privileged class, an excuse or reason for failure or lack of achievement. Master morality takes all the blame for their own lack of success whereas the slave morality assigns all the blame of their lack of success upon an oppressor or privileged class or master.

Nietzsche said in his book the Anti-Christ "The most spiritual men, as the strongest, find their happiness where others would find their destruction: in the labyrinth, in hardness against themselves and others, in experiments. Their joy is self-conquest: asceticism becomes in them nature, need, and instinct. Difficult tasks are a privilege to them; to play with burdens that crush others, a recreation. Knowledge-a form of asceticism. They are the most venerable kind of man: that does not preclude they're being the most cheerful and the kindliest."

Nietzsche said, "The change form master morality to slave morality has dared to invert the aristocratic value equation of good, noble, powerful, beautiful, happy, favored-of-the-gods and maintain, with the furious hatred of the underprivileged and impotent, that "only the poor, the powerless, the oppressed, the victims are good; only the suffering, sick, and ugly, are truly blessed. But you noble and mighty ones of the earth will be, brought down for all eternity, cursed and damned!" For to be a powerful successful, happy, self-reliant master is to be evil, and cruel, and avaricious, we must fight against you".

For a slave being Worthy of pity is more valuable than being worthy of praise. Worthy of protection is more important than being so strong you don't need protection.
We even have special protected classes those with extra and special rights and privileges because they are too weak to protect or care for themselves and these groups are glorified.
Nietzsche said the ones of slave morality they cry for a good opinion of themselves by others because they are not able to set their own value. They want others

to value them, to do community work, common work to be seen by others as good or kind or nice. Nietzsche said the one with slave morality "His soul squints; his mind loves hide-outs, secret paths, and back doors; everything that is hidden seems to him his own world, his security, his comfort; he is expert in silence, in long memory, in waiting, in provisional self-depreciation, and in self-humiliation. Hypocrisy is not just a trait of those with Slave Morality it is their very essence. They must pretend they are strong and free and their weakness and cowardice is a free choice."

Nietzsche said "As is well known, the priests are the most evil enemies—but why? Because they are the most impotent. It is because of their impotence that in them hatred grows to monstrous and uncanny proportions, to the most spiritual and poisonous kind of hatred. The truly great haters in world history have always been priests; likewise, the most ingenious haters: other kinds of spirit hardly come into consideration when compared with the spirit of priestly vengefulness."

Nietzsche was very clear in the contrast between slave morality and master morality with master morality you killed your enemies if someone had done you wrong you challenged them to a duel which might be a pistol or sword fight this was common for all free men… but a slave did not have this option so began the concept of forgive your enemies. Now this is preposterous to a free man and unnatural and illogic thing. If someone slaps your face you turn and offer him the other side of your face to slap. If someone murders your children you forgive them because someone else god or the state will punish them. Being unable to avenge has been twisted by the slave to choosing not to. A slave now chooses to be happy with his lot his lack of choice a slave is happy with his lack of revenge a slave is happy with his lack of freedom this Nietzsche says has produced a new form of morality which he called Slave morality.

The "wellborn" really felt that they were also the "happy." They did not have to construct their happiness factitiously by looking at their enemies, as all rancorous men are wont to do, and being fully active, energetic people, they were incapable of divorcing happiness from action. They accounted activity a necessary part of happiness (which explains the origin of the phrase eu prattein).

All this stands in utter contrast to what is called happiness among the impotent and oppressed, who are full of bottled-up aggressions. Their happiness is purely passive and takes the form of drugged tranquility, stretching and yawning, peace, "sabbath," emotional slackness. Whereas the noble lives before his own conscience with confidence and frankness (~gennaios "nobly bred" emphasizes the nuance "truthful" and perhaps also "ingenuous"), the rancorous person is neither truthful nor ingenuous nor honest and forthright with himself. His soul squints; his mind loves hide-outs, secret paths, and back doors; everything that is hidden seems to him his own world, his security, his comfort; he is expert in silence, in long memory, in waiting, in provisional self-depreciation, and in self-humiliation.

Nietzsche said "When a noble man feels resentment, it is absorbed in his instantaneous reaction and therefore does not poison him. Moreover, in countless cases where we might expect it, it never arises, while with weak and impotent people it occurs without fail. It is a sign of strong, rich temperaments that they cannot for long take seriously their enemies, their misfortunes, their misdeeds; for such characters have in them an excess of plastic curative power, and also a power of oblivion. (A good modern example of the latter is Mirabeau, who lacked all memory for insults and meannesses done him, and who was unable to forgive because he had forgotten). Such a man simply shakes off vermin which would get beneath another's skin—and only here, if anywhere on earth, is it possible to speak of "loving one's enemy."

Nietzsche said "As we all know, priests are the most evil enemies to have why should this be so? Because they are the most impotent. It is their impotence which makes their haste so violent and sinister, so cerebral and poisonous. The greatest haters in history" "This was a strategy entirely appropriate to a priestly people in whom vindictiveness had gone most deeply underground. It was the Jew who, with frightening consistency, dared to invert the aristocratic value equations good/noble/powerful/beautiful/happy/favored-of-the-gods and maintain, with the furious hatred of the underprivileged and impotent, that "only the poor, the powerless, are good; only the suffering, sick, and ugly, truly blessed. But you noble and mighty ones of the earth will be, to all eternity, the evil, the cruel, the avaricious, the godless, and thus the cursed and damned!"

And could one, by straining every resource, hit upon a bait more dangerous than this? What could equal in debilitating narcotic power the symbol of the "holy cross," the ghastly paradox of a crucified god, the unspeakably cruel mystery of God's self-crucifixion for the benefit of mankind? One thing is certain, that in this sign Israel has by now triumphed over all other, nobler values.

What accounts for our repugnance to man—for there is no question that he makes us suffer? Certainly not our fear of him, rather the fact that there is no longer anything to be feared from him; that the vermin "man" occupies the entire stage; that, tame, hopelessly mediocre, and savorless, he considers himself the apex of historical evolution; and not entirely without justice, since he is still somewhat removed from the mass of sickly and effete creatures whom Europe is beginning to stink of today.

Here I want to give vent to a sigh and a last hope. Exactly what is it that I, especially, find intolerable; that I am unable to cope with; that asphyxiates me? A bad smell. The smell of failure, of a soul that has gone stale. God knows it is possible to endure all kinds of misery— vile weather, sickness, trouble, isolation. All this can be coped with, if one is born to a life of anonymity and battle. There will always be moments of re-emergence into the light, when one tastes the golden hour of victory and once again stands foursquare, unshakable, and ready to face even harder things, like a bowstring drawn taut against new perils. But, you divine patronesses—if there are any such in the realm beyond good and evil—

Another Nietzsche quote is this. To expect that strength will not manifest itself as strength, that it must not consist of a will to overpower, a will to throw down, a will to rule, a thirst for enemies and opposition and triumph as the desire to overcome, is every bit as absurd as to expect that weakness will manifest itself as strength, the urge to compete, to conquer, to overcome obstacles to fight, to struggle to stand alone against great odds to declare yourself sovereign." A quantum of strength is equivalent to a quantum of urge, will, activity, and it is only the snare of language (of the arch-fallacies of reason petrified in language), presenting all activity as conditioned by an agent—the "subject"—that blinds us to this fact. For, just as popular superstition divorces the lightning from its brilliance, viewing the latter as an activity whose subject is the lightning, so does popular morality divorce strength from its manifestations, as though there were behind the strong a neutral agent, free to manifest its strength or contain it? But no such agent exists; there is no "being" behind the doing, acting, becoming; the "doer" has simply been added to the deed by the imagination—the doing is everything. The common man actually doubles the doing by making the lightning flash; he states the same event once as cause and then again as effect. The natural scientists are no better when they say that "energy moves," "energy causes." For all its detachment and freedom from emotion, our science is still the dupe of linguistic habits; it has never yet got rid of those changelings called "subjects." The atom is one such changeling, another is the Kantian "thing-in-itself." Small wonder, then, that the repressed and smoldering emotions of vengeance and hatred have taken advantage of this superstition and in fact espouse no belief more ardently than that it is within the discretion of the strong to be weak, of the bird of prey to be a lamb. Thus, they assume the right of calling the bird of prey to account for being a bird of prey. We can hear the oppressed, downtrodden, violated whispering among themselves with the wily vengefulness of the impotent, "Let us be unlike those evil ones. Let us be good. And the good shall be he who does not do violence, does not attack or retaliate, who leaves vengeance to God, who, like us, lives hidden, who shuns all that is evil, and altogether asks very little of life like us, the patient, the humble, the just ones." Read in cold blood, this means nothing more than "We weak ones are, in fact, weak. It is a good thing that we do nothing for which we are not strong enough." But this plain fact, this basic prudence, which even the insects have (who, in circumstances of great danger, sham death in order not to have to "do" too much) has tricked itself out in the garb of quiet, virtuous resignation, thanks to the duplicity of impotence—as though the weakness of the weak, which is after all his essence, his natural way of being, his sole and inevitable reality, were a spontaneous act, a meritorious deed. This sort of person requires the belief in a "free subject" able to choose indifferently, out of that instinct of self-preservation which notoriously justifies every kind of lie. It may well be that to this day the subject, or in popular language the soul, has been the most viable of all articles of faith simply because it makes it possible for the majority of mankind—i.e., the weak and oppressed of every sort—to practice the sublime sleight of hand which gives weakness the appearance of free choice and one's natural disposition the distinction of merit.

Fredrick Nietzsche was a truth seeker he believed that most people were dumb, lazy, ignorant and had fallen into a weak pathetic state of self-delusion. He called religion the opiate of the masses, and thought most people where hypocrites speaking of peace and loving their enemies while killing and attacking them in underhanded ways to avoid open fighting. Nietzsche despised this and said you are not entitled to isolated thoughts. Your thoughts must be one tree, whole, one root, one trunk, one limb, one fruit. The image of a person being a Christian and vengeful was a breakdown in logic to him. He described these people as rancorous. Full of conflicting ideas, beliefs, hypocrisy and poison.

Nietzsche thought it funny that those with no ability to defend themselves would say not defending themselves is a virtue when they had no other choice. Another thing among the many which made Nietzsche such an amazing thinker was he said those with Master Morality should own up to envy. Envy is a notice that you can do better or should have more and that you want more. It's a friend reminding you of what you should have. If you envy you are inadequate and should be doing better. It's a good reminder of what you should have done. What you should become. Those with Slave morality would not have envy and would consider it bad because they cannot make any more. They can only have what is given to them by a master. If they want more they must be good slaves and hope a master how might give them more. Which is similar to what the democrats hope the government will do give them more. Christianity protects people from their envy which is bad according to Nietzsche. Communism does the same which is also bad and in many countries Communism has replaced religion because it is such a close match.

Slave morality denounces what it wants but can't have
Master Morality recognizes what it wants and works to
acquire it.
You can see many other examples of the twisting
traits as viewed from the paradigm of slave morality
or master morality.
1, Sexlessness became purity
2, Submission to people you hate becomes obedience
3, Weakness becomes goodness
4, Not being able to take revenge becomes
forgiveness
Christianity a machine of bitter denial lies of
resentment and bottled up aggressions

Nietzsche believed the two great narcotics in European
society were Christianity and alcohol both numb you
to pain and make you content with being a loser.
While Christianity has diminished as a narcotic for
western society as Christianity is losing ground rapidly
to atheism but in giving up the god of Christianity
those with slave morality have replaced it with
Communism, Socialism, Collectivistism worship of the
collective or Statetheism which is worship of the
State. In some modern people with slave mentality
Government has become a god to worship, have faith
in, and pay tribute to.

Again, I am humbled by Nietzsche who in Thus spoke Zarathustra said this about parasites and the weak helpless living off the strong.

"Where the strong are weak, where the noble are all-too-gentle--there buildeth it its loathsome nest; the parasite liveth where the great have small sore-places.

What is the highest of all species of being, and what is the lowest? The parasite is the lowest species; he, however, who is of the highest species feedeth most parasites.

For the soul which hath the longest ladder, and can go deepest down: how could there fail to be most parasites upon it?

It is out of the deepest depth that the highest high must come to its height

--The most comprehensive soul, which can run and stray and rove furthest in itself; the most necessary soul, which out of joy flingeth itself into chance.

--The soul in Being, which plungeth into Becoming; the possessing soul, which SEEKETH to attain desire and longing: --

--The soul fleeing from itself, which overtaketh itself in the widest circuit; the wisest soul, unto which folly speaketh most sweetly:--

--The soul most self-loving, in which all things have their current and counter-current, their ebb and their flow: --oh, how could THE LOFTIEST SOUL fail to have the worst parasites?

Those are enough Nietzsche quotes to give you a taste of what his perspective was. I would encourage you to read his books for yourself.

Chapter 10
No peaceful solution

We have 2 distinct groups of people who can barely exist in peace together. One with master mentality and one with slave mentality. The master sees the slave as a man sees a tapeworm, it is a parasite that is doing him harm out to injure him and must be removed. The other with slave mentality which sees the master as an object that must be subdued, taxed, feed off of and attacked because it is oppressive. Those with slave morality see those with master morality as one who has undeserved and stolen status and goods as a thief who must be punished. One that must be reduced to a slave. This is not different than the Master Moral people because the Slave Moral people act as if those with Master Morals are a host that must be fed on and brought down. But this is a conflict for those with Slave Morality because the oppressor is needed for the oppressed to even have existence

These events were so polarizing because 2 vastly different types of people with 2 vastly different types of thinking given the same set of data and facts came to 2 vastly different conclusions.

These two moralities as Nietzsche said two hundred years ago cannot exist together. Each will hate and seek to destroy the other. If we look at the list of moral traits each side admires we can see how incompatible this situation is. I see no way for these 2 ways to peacefully coexist. One must consume the other.

Chapter 11
Masters Lie and Deceive

I originally wrote this as a response to a person on Facebook during the 2016 election. It grew too large to post on Facebook so I just wrote it as one of my essays. And stuck it in a long list with hundreds of others. But after sharing it with 2 people I highly respect, who are very harsh critics and who never praise anything told me they liked it. I decided to try to do a short little book. After showing it to some other people I was surprised that many people found it so easily digestible and understandable. However, a couple people who found it very understandable said to me I understand everything you wrote I just can't understand why the very rich and powerful have slave morality. Why do all the Hollywood millionaires, the actors the rich and powerful, the Bill Gates, and Mark Zuckerberg, and the college professors, why do they push for a slave morality agenda.

I told them those people are not slave minded and they don't have slave morality. Those people have Master morality and want to be the masters. And so according to the morality the more people they can turn into slaves and the farther they can spread slave morality and the more people they can get to adopt slave mentality the more powerful they will be. I explained that every millionaire who wants to make guns illegal for the citizens has armed bodyguards carrying guns. That every millionaire who wants illegal immigrants allowed in with the citizens of this country lives in a gated community were no illegal immigrant or any immigrant will ever set foot on their property. I explained that those millionaires with master morality are never harmed by competing with low wage jobs by illegal immigrants. I explained that the millionaires who fly private jets never have to worry about airport security. The millionaires who want all the funding for special programs for public schools never send their kids to those public schools, their kids will always go to a private school. Their kids will have armed bodyguards. Their kids will be in a safe neighborhood behind gates and fences, the very same people who don't want a wall or border around the country have a wall or fence or border around their property.

It is those who act like prey who are the most dangerous predators. The very same people in Hollywood who are rich and famous will never lose their money or fame by telling the masses to act like slaves. The rich and famous masters of Hollywood gain more riches and fame by telling everyone to be slaves and promoting slave morality. I did not realize that this clarification showing the sharp division of those with master morality versus those with slave morality would need further clarification by explaining that many masters tell slaves to be good slaves and that they will do things for them and that it is right to be a slave a dutiful slave and that we should all be slaves.

This does not mean that the masters those with master morality believe it for themselves. So that is why Al Gore flies in a private jet and has a carbon footprint of 100 ordinary Americans but tells everyone else to use less carbon. Or any Hollywood actress with 10 mansions says America should let in all the refugees but her 10 mansions stay empty. They are promoting slave morality but that does not mean they have slave morality themselves. Look back in history all masters have promoted slave morality. Masters want slave morality for the masses. Do you really think George Soros has slave morality? Do you really think the millionaire stars who made it have slave morality? Just by watching the rich and powerful act vs what the rich and powerful do will let you know what hypocrites they are.

Chapter 12
Fear for the Future

I was listening to some women talking about how scared they were for the future. They said Trump is going to get us into a war, they said a crazy unbalanced man has his finger on the nuclear button. They were very concerned that this maniac, monster is now leading the United States. One of them had even taken part in the resistance marches. One of these women had even sent out an email to her coworkers explaining how we all must work together now and help each other and gather our loved ones close because Trump was elected president. She did not seem to comprehend that if she had sent out the same email in 2008 when Obama had been elected she probably would have been fired for racism.

I said I am very worried Trump's presidency also. They looked at me and said I wouldn't expect you to be worried about this. I said no just like you and maybe more than you I'm very concerned about Trump being president but probably for the opposite reason you are. They did not seem to understand this and ask what I meant. I said the great Nietzsche said, "Be careful when you battle monsters that you don't become a monster."
"When you stare into the abyss long enough the abyss stares back at you"
"thoughts are things and we create our own reality".
All I hear now is Trump is horrible, Trump is a racist, Trump is a Nazi, Americas full of racists, Americas full of Nazis, Americas full white supremacists, Cops are shooting black people for no reason. Trump hates woman, women aren't being paid as much as man for the exact same job. Are you really working that hard to make those things come true?

Trump is being attacked at every turn, by every media outlet, by every news agency. Every Hollywood actor, every Yahoo! News story, any news outlet that can put out anything about Trump's shoes his wife's shoes his eating ice cream his children is the most negative vicious attack any president has ever endured. And these attacks are not by one or 2 individuals they are by million-dollar corporations. Every time I point out the unfair attacks on Trump I will have some dishonest person show one poor hillbilly in Appalachia who had assigned saying he disliked Obama that is nothing compared to Meryl Streep getting up in the global Golden globes with a million viewers making an articulate speech against Trump. So, I have a couple concerns one is that anyone would eventually crack under this pressure. Do you really want to drive this person to push the nuclear button do you really want to attack this person so much that they just say I do hate this entire country and want to destroy it? Is that the reality you want to create? So, I have a very grave concern. That the country is treating a powerful individual so horribly that they might eventually retaliate if you scream at me 1000 times that I'm going to punch you in the nose. You might do it long enough so that I eventually want to punch you in the nose and do punch you in the nose I can see Trump cracking under a nonstop for your attack and doing that.

The other danger I see is that you were also doing that the half of the country that voted for him. I've never heard of a Nazi or white supremacist until Charlottesville. I don't think they got much press I don't think there very many members of the KKK but if you keep fanning the flames and saying everyone is a racist, everyone is a member of the KKK, everyone is a white supremacist you can grow that. I don't think the monster you want to exist does exist but if you keep creating that monster and feeding that monster and nurturing that monster you will create that monster.

So, I have 2 concerns one that the incredible palpable hatred toward trump might manifest itself to turn him into a monster. The Catholics used to pray for the president to be helped and guided by god to make good decisions. Well the United States of America is doing exactly the opposite with Trump so if thoughts are things and there is any validity the psychic spiritual or mental energy it could certainly turn him into a monster. No leader in the earth's history has had more negative spiritual, psychic energy thought and prayer send his way. And secondly, I think the sides lining up to fight is insane. America already had one Civil War in which more Americans were killed than all the other wars put together. World War 2 was far less damaging to America than our Civil war. Yet the reasons to fight the first Civil war were so small compared to the reasons to fight the second civil war. About 2% of men in the south owned slaves. And for a poor man in the south to support slavery was stupid beyond belief. But it happened. And why did any free men in the north volunteer to be maimed and killed to stop slavery. General Grant the Norths great general owned slaves. He didn't care about freeing slaves. And General Lee the Souths great general didn't own any slaves. Yet the nation was dumped into a horrible fight. Wars can start over the dumbest things. Look at World War I. There was no reason for it. And certainly, no reason for America to get involved in it. So, given the track record of the past. America has more of a logical reason to get into a Civil War now that in did in the first Civil war or World War I

I do think that the 2020 election will be a bloodbath and make the 2016 election look like a lovefest. We already have battle lines being drawn up and YouTube, Facebook, internet providers all trying to censor and stop one side from speaking. And if speaking is not allowed fighting is the next recourse. You love it when a speaker at a college is shut down. You love it when a group of people who want to preserve civil war monuments are shut down labeled Nazis and beaten bloody. You love it when the internet takes away peoples YouTube channels. But you don't seem to realize the pendulum swings both ways and the farther you push it one direction the harder it will swing back.

www.ingramcontent.com/pod-product-compliance
Lightning Source LLC
Chambersburg PA
CBHW051233250726
48655CB00006B/2755